Join our Facebook group Healthy Hustlers!

Go to FB and search: Healthy Hustlers

This group is a place for both men and women to start their journey towards a healthier lifestyle! A place where we can support each other, share workout plans, recipes, meal planning, inspiration etc. Mike and I start workout routines, detoxes or any health goal together. It helps you stay on track when you have a support system to push you!

www.mbpowercouple.com

About Brandy...#entrepreneur #naturalmama

I'm a busy work from home mama to a LARGE blended family, our youngest is 17 months old!! It's very important to me that our family eats healthy, home cooked meals no matter how busy we are. I wrote this cookbook to share with you that eating healthy doesn't have to be difficult.

I've always loved to cook. When I was a teenager my parents worked a lot so it was my job to make dinner. I was making Pot Roasts at 14 years old!! As I've continued on with my journey to a healthier lifestyle I've taught myself how to make the comfort foods we all love with a healthier twist.

Eating healthy doesn't have to be boring!! In this book I will share with you both mine and my family's favorite recipes along with some of the products and supplements we love. I'll also give you a list of the items we like to buy when we grocery shop and where I usually purchase them.

It's a Passion...

I'm a mom on a mission to keep my family healthy in this very toxic world we live in! Toxins and chemicals are EVERYWHERE! From the food we eat, the products we use to clean our clothes and our homes, even our skincare products are full of harmful ingredients.

I've transitioned our house to as chemical free as possible and I hope to help you do the same with this book. My goal is to provide you with easy, non-gmo, organic meals your family will love. As well as easy recipes to make your own nontoxic cleaning supplies at home.

Remember it won't happen overnight and every little change makes a BIG difference! It's easy to start with small changes like swapping out your scented plug-ins with essential oil diffusers and making your own cleaning sprays. Starting to read labels and learn what is actually in your food will make a big difference in your grocery trips (although shopping may take you a bit longer) Staying away from added sugars, artificial ingredients and processed foods are easy changes to make.

Cover Story... #momlife

My good friend Orville Mceachron came over to do photos in our kitchen for the cover of this book 2 days before Christmas. We had 5 of our children involved that day and it was chaotic!!! My 10 year old was cranky and didn't want to participate. When half the kids were listening the others weren't! Typical day with kid's right?!?! Orville wasn't happy with any of the pics so he ended up coming back the next day.....Christmas Eve to start over.

We threatened the kids with every chore known to mankind that they better cooperate this time......and they did!! We got beautiful pictures that were literally picture perfect and will hang in our house at some point. But as much as I love those pictures I went with one from the first day. One where my 10 year old looks annoyed and my 12 year old has marks in his hair because he didn't want to take off his hat. This is what our life really looks like. Not staged, slightly messy and a little crazy. This is real life. My life isn't picture perfect so this book isn't either! I hope you enjoy it.

Connect with Orville at www.cleweekly.com

I hope you love my recipes!

Brandy

Taco Shells *"Taco night brings the (blended) family together!"*

"I'm getting the hang of making these tacos! Fun, Simple & easy for this busy, full-time working mom AND my kids love them!" ~Nicole Lemire

- Corn Tortillas (we love sprouted corn tortillas)
- Avocado or Coconut Oil (higher smoke point)
- Garlic Salt
- Limes (optional but highly recommended)

1. Fill a small frying pan with oil and turn on medium heat*
2. Add 1 tortilla and cook on both sides until lightly crispy
3. Remove from oil and fold in half with 2 forks to create a shell
4. Sprinkle with garlic salt to taste
5. Half of our house likes to top our taco shells with fresh lime juice

*Depending if you are using electric or gas stove, you may have to play with the correct temperature setting to set the oil for optimal cooking of your shells. We use medium heat on a gas stove.

We usually go through a ton of tacos on taco night so add more oil to your pan as needed. We like our tacos with ground turkey or my crockpot whole chicken, black beans, cheese, avocado, tomatoes, Sriracha and lactose free sour cream.

Tortellini Soup

- 5 Mason jars (12 oz jars) of homemade Bone Broth
- 4 Mason jars (12 oz jars) water
- 1 Package Organic frozen Spinach
- 1 Package ground sausage (buy local)
- 1 Can Organic tomatoes
- 2 Packages Tortellini (use 1 cheese and 1 mushroom)
- 4 Cloves Garlic
- ½ Inch piece turmeric root
- 1 Stalk Leeks chopped
- 2 TBSP Coconut Oil
- Provolone Cheese (optional)

Broth:
Combine bone broth, water, leeks, turmeric, coconut oil and garlic in large stock pan and simmer 2-3 hours.
Strain garlic cloves, turmeric and leeks from broth after cooking and discard

1. Cook sausage in frying pan and drain
2. Cook tortellini and rinse with cold water
3. Add frozen spinach, tomatoes and sausage to stock pot
4. Simmer for 1-2 hours.
5. Add cooked tortellini
6. Serve topped with provolone (optional)

Crockpot Whole Chicken

"Our 5 year old loves it so much he made his mom make it!"

I love making a whole chicken in my crockpot! Not only does it make an easy dinner but I save the homemade chicken stock for future recipes and I make bone broth out of the carcass
(See bone broth recipe)

1 Whole Chicken (we like to buy ours from a local farm but if that's not an option make sure you get one that is grass-fed, hormone and antibiotic free)

- 2-6 Cloves Garlic
- Handful Fresh Rosemary
- Handful Fresh Sage
- Handful Fresh Thyme
- Sea Salt, Black Pepper and Turmeric to taste

1. Stuff chicken with garlic, rosemary, sage and thyme
2. Put in crockpot on low for 6-8 hours or high for 4 hours if in a time crunch
3. Season top of chicken with turmeric, sea salt and black pepper
4. Chicken will create its own natural broth so no need to add water
5. Baste with broth while it cooks
6. Before serving remove broth and put in mason jars for later use *I let the broth cool on the counter before freezing it

Roasted Cabbage

"You will be surprised at how much KIDS love this!!"

- 1 Organic head of cabbage
- Avocado oil
- Garlic salt
- Turmeric
- Pepper

1. Preheat oven to 400 degrees
2. Drizzle avocado oil on baking dish
3. Cut cabbage into roughly ½ inch segments
4. Lay out on baking sheet
5. Drizzle olive oil over top
6. Season with garlic salt, turmeric and black pepper
7. Roast until brown on bottom then flip and cook the other side

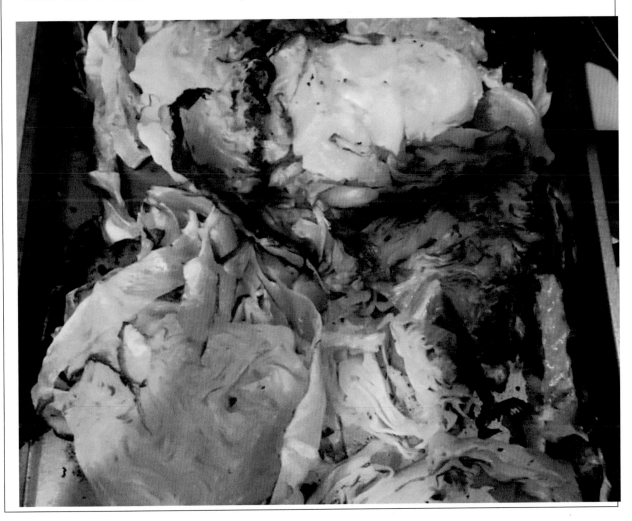

Chocolate Peanut Butter Fat Bomb

- ½ Cup natural peanut butter
- ½ Cup organic, unrefined coconut oil
- ¼ Cup cacao powder
- 1/3 Cup local honey (I purchase from a local farm)
- ¼ TSP Sea salt

1. Melt peanut butter, coconut oil and cacao powder on low in small pan
2. Remove from heat, add honey and sea salt
3. Pour into silicone molds and refrigerate until set
4. Remove from molds and store in an airtight container in refrigerator

When it's "that time of the month" I crave chocolate like CRAZY!! These are an awesome guilt free snack!! Just don't eat 5 of them like I do!! ;)

Crock Pot Mac 'n Cheese

"I want more, says every child here!"

- 1 Box Organic Cavatelli
- 1 Package Kerrygold Blarney Castle Cheese
- 1 Package Kerrygold Aged Cheddar
- ¼ Cup Kerrygold Butter
- 3 Cups Almond Milk
- Pink Sea Salt, Garlic, Black Pepper, Turmeric to taste

Here is how to make it:

1. Boil pasta until almost done, you want it slightly al dente
2. Cut cheese into cubes
3. Combine all ingredients in crockpot
4. Season with sea salt, garlic, black pepper and turmeric
5. Let cook 2-3 hours on low, stirring occasionally

Carrot Cake Overnight Oats

Easy make ahead breakfast!!

- ½ Cup sprouted oats
- ½ Cup unsweetened flax milk or almond milk
- 2 TBSP plain yogurt
- 1 TBSP raisins
- 1 TBSP maple syrup
- ¼ TSP ground cinnamon
- ½ Scoop vanilla protein powder
- ⅛ TSP ground nutmeg
- 1 TBSP chopped walnuts
- ¼ Cup shredded carrots

1. Add oats to mason jar
2. Then add flax milk, carrot, yogurt, protein powder raisins, maple syrup, cinnamon, nutmeg & walnuts
3. Refrigerate overnight or at least for 5 hours
4. When ready to eat, stir well
5. Enjoy warm or cold

Blackberry Coconut Fat Bombs!

- 1 Cup coconut oil
- 1/3 Cup Kerrygold butter
- 1 Package fresh blackberries
- ½ Scoop vanilla meal replacement powder
- 2 TBSP collagen peptides
- 4-6 TBSP local honey
- 3 TBSP unsweetened coconut flakes

Fat Bombs are like energy balls but made almost exclusively from high -fat, low-carb ingredients. Unsaturated healthy fats are really good for you and these little bombs taste great!

1. Melt coconut oil and butter on low heat
2. Combine vanilla meal replacement powder, blackberries, collagen peptides, coconut flakes, and coconut-butter
3. Mix in a blender
4. Add honey and mix again
5. Pour into silicone molds and refrigerate until set
6. Store in fridge and enjoy!

Cauliflower Sketti

Great meal for anyone gluten free!

- 1 Bag shredded cauliflower (or chop your own)
- 1 Zucchini
- Spaghetti sauce
- Avocado oil
- Mozzarella cheese

1. Brown shredded cauliflower in skillet with avocado oil
2. Add Zucchini and cook on low
3. Cook 10-15 minutes or until zucchini is soft
4. Add sauce and stir
5. Top with mozzarella cheese and seasonings of your choice and serve

Zucchini Lasagna

"So cheesy and good they won't even miss the noodles!"

Ingredients:

2-4 \ Zucchini thinly sliced in place of lasagna noodles
Organic marinara sauce
Local ground chicken or turkey
Ricotta cheese
Mozzarella cheese
Organic spinach
Organic orange and yellow peppers chopped small
2-3 Garlic cloves minced
Turmeric
Rosemary
Garlic
Black pepper
Pink sea salt
Paper towels

1. Preheat oven to 350 degrees
2. Thinly slice zucchini
3. Lay paper towels out on counter and spread zucchini slices out
4. Sprinkle with sea salt and place another paper towel on top.
5. Let sit for 15-20 minutes to draw out some of the moisture
6. Spread sauce on bottom of baking dish
7. Arrange zucchini slices over sauce
8. Layer meat, garlic, ricotta, spinach, peppers and mozzarella
9. Top with a layer of zucchini
10. Spread sauce over zucchini
11. Top with mozzarella cheese, turmeric, rosemary, garlic, black   pepper and sea salt
12. Bake for 35-40 minutes. Cool for 20 minutes before serving

Are you a vegetarian? Leave out the meat

Asian Salmon

Wild caught salmon filets

Marinade:
1/3 Cup toasted sesame oil
1/3 Cup coconut aminos
1-2 Cloves minced garlic
1/3 Cup Avocado oil
½-1 TBSP grated ginger
¼ Cup local honey

1. Combine all ingredients and pour over salmon
2. Let marinate for a few hours in fridge
3. Cook at 400 in baking dish and baste with sauce while cooking

"This is great choice for DATE night!"

White Chicken Chili

Hearty and healthy winter dish!

- 1 Pound organic chicken breasts
- 3 15 oz Cans great northern beans
- 4 oz Cans chopped green chilies
- 1 Minced jalapeno
- 4 Cloves garlic minced
- 1 Stalk leeks chopped
- 1/1/2 TSP cumin
- 1 Lime juiced
- Salt, pepper, dried oregano
- 4-6 12 oz Mason jars bone broth
- ½ Cup almond milk
- 2 TBSP GF flour, I used Arrowroot flour

1. Add all ingredients together in crockpot
2. Cook on low for 4 hours
3. Remove chicken and shred, add back into crockpot
4. Whisk together milk and flour in small dish then stir into chili
5. Cover and cook 30-40 minutes
6. Top with shredded cheese, sour cream and crushed tortillas

Zucchini Chips

"The kids will never want unhealthy chips again."

- 1-3 Zucchini
- Oil (we use avocado oil)
- Salt
- Pepper
- Hot sauce (optional)

Here is how to make it:

1. Thinly slice zucchini
2. Dry the slices between 2 paper towels to extract moisture
3. Lightly press on it while drying (dry 10-15 min)
4. Brush with oil
5. Lightly sprinkle with salt and pepper
6. Bake for 2+ hours at 225 or until crisp

Betcha you can't just eat ONE!!

Guilt Free Apple Crisp

- 1 Cup sprouted oats
- 1/2 Cup coconut flour
- 1/2 Cup chopped walnuts
- 3/4 TSP cinnamon
- 1/4 TSP sea salt
- 1/4 Cup pure maple syrup
- 1/4 Cup melted Kerrygold butter

1. Cut apples, put in crockpot on low with local honey and cinnamon.
2. Combine, oats, flour, walnuts, sea salt, maple syrup, butter (use bowl)
3. Once mixed together pour over apples.
4. Cover with paper towel (to draw out moisture)
5. Cook 15-30 min.

Serve warm and enjoy!

Peanut Butter Banana Smoothie

- 1 Banana
- 4-6 Ounces almond milk
- 2 TBSP Natural peanut butter
- 1 Scoop vanilla protein powder
- 1 Scoop Cocoa Superfood
- 2-3 Medjool dates
- Ice

Combine all ingredients in a blender or magic bullet, blend and enjoy!

I also suggest adding your favorite supplements or superfoods!

KID APPROVED!!!

Turmeric Tea

- 1 Gallon Water
- 3 Organic lemons (juiced, add juice and lemons)
- 1 Organic cinnamon stick
- 1 Inch piece of organic ginger root
- 1/2-1 TBSP Organic ground turmeric
- Dash of black pepper
- Local honey
- 1 Clove (optional)

1. Add all ingredients together in a large pot
2. Bring to a boil then simmer for 45 min to an hour
3. Let cool then add 1/2-1 cup local honey

Enjoy hot or cold!

Asian Noodle Soup

- 3 Medium mason jars of bone broth
- 1 Package rice noodles
- Wild Shrimp
- 1 Cup chopped mushrooms
- 2 TBS chopped fresh cilantro
- 1 Lime juice
- 2 Garlic cloves
- Dash of coconut aminos
- 1 1/2 Avocado diced
- 1 Cup chopped Kale
- 2 TBSP coconut oil

1. Cook rice noodles in water, drain and rinse
2. Boil raw shrimp until pink then drain and rinse
3. In big pot combine bone broth, garlic, mushrooms, kale, cilantro and cooked shrimp. Turn on med-low
4. Add cooked noodles, lime juice and avocado
5. Salt and pepper to taste and serve!

Fried Rice

"Who needs take out?!"

- 2 Cups basmati rice
- 2 ½ Cups bone broth or chicken broth
- Chopped ham or chicken
- 1 Carrot (diced)
- 2 Cloves garlic
- Handful fresh cilantro (chopped)
- Avocado oil
- Lime
- 2 Eggs (whisked)
- Turmeric, pink sea salt and black pepper

1. Add broth and rice to rice cooker
2. Sautéed carrots, garlic and cilantro in wok with oil
3. Add meat and 2 eggs, and continue to cook until meat is browned and eggs are slightly cooked
4. Add rice and cook another 10ish minutes
5. Finish with turmeric, pink sea salt, black pepper and lime juice

Pumpkin Chocolate Cookies

"You will never buy packaged cookie dough again."

- **1 Cup organic pumpkin puree**
- **½ Cup organic unrefined coconut oil**
- **1 Egg**
- **1 Cup coconut sugar**
- **1 TSP organic vanilla**
- **2 TBSP almond or coconut milk (unsweetened)**
- **1 Cup coconut flour**
- **2 TSP cinnamon**
- **½ TSP pink sea salt**
- **2 Cups chocolate chips (try Enjoy Life for dairy free)**
- **2 TSP pumpkin pie spice**

1. **Combine coconut oil, pumpkin puree, sugar, egg, and vanilla**
2. **Combine cinnamon, salt and flour in a separate bowl**
3. **Add flour mix to pumpkin mixture**
4. **Add milk**
5. **Fold in chocolate chips**
6. **Preheat oven to 350**
7. **Scoop onto cookie sheet**
8. **Bake for 10-12 minutes**
9. **Store in refrigerator**

Bone Broth

"Amazing for gut health and the perfect base for any soup!"

- Carcass from a whole chicken
- Water
- 1-2 TBSP Apple Cider Vinegar
- 2-6 Cloves of garlic
- ½ Inch piece of fresh turmeric root
- Black pepper
- Onion (optional)
- Leeks (optional)
- Carrots (optional)
- 2 TBSP Coconut oil (add at end)

Bone Broth is incredibly nutritious and is amazing for so many things, such as gut health, strengthening your immune system, improve digestive issues, remineralize teeth and so much more! It's high in the amino acids proline and glycine which are vital for healthy connective tissues. It's also one of the world's best sources of natural collagen. Bone broth is great to drink on its own and to use as a base for soups.

1. Make a whole chicken for dinner, pick all the remaining meat off and leave the carcass
2. Add chop leeks, carrots, celery and onion
3. Peel garlic and throw cloves in whole (5)
4. Peel turmeric root and throw in whole
5. Add apple cider vinegar
6. Fill crockpot to top with water
7. Cook on low for 24 hours (chicken bones) or 48 hours (beef bones)
8. Let cool slightly then strain and store. I keep mine in the freezer in mason jars

Smashed Berries "Syrup"

We stopped buying syrup after we discovered this!

1 cup frozen organic raspberries

1 cup frozen organic strawberries

1. Heat on low in small saucepan

2. Smash berries as they thaw

3. Serve over pancakes

KID APPROVED!!!

Blackberry Goat Cheese Pizza

Trust me and try it!!

- Udi's Gluten Free Pizza Crust (see shopping list)
- Goat Cheese (see shopping list)
- Spinach
- Kerrygold Butter
- Garlic Salt
- Blackberries

1. Spread Kerrygold on frozen pizza crust
2. Sprinkle with garlic salt
3. Smash blackberries in a bowl
4. Layer spinach, goat cheese and smashed blackberries
5. Bake at 375* for 15 minutes

Banana Pancakes

"Throw out that boxed stuff now!"

- 1 Banana
- 1 Egg
- 1 Scoop Vanilla protein powder
- 1 TSP Cinnamon
- 1 Cup sprouted oats
- Avocado Oil
- 1/2 Cup almond milk
- Blend together and pour onto hot, oiled skillet

"Oh my goodness! Absolutely delicious! These take pancakes to a whole new level and oh so healthy! Adult and kid approved! So easy to make!" ~Laura Spencer, Ohio

Oven "Fried" Chicken

- Organic chicken legs and thighs
- Arrowroot flour
- Turmeric, pink sea salt & pepper
- 2 eggs
- Large zip lock bag
- Avocado oil

1. Beat eggs
2. Fill zip lock with flour
3. Dip chicken in eggs an shake in bag of flour
4. Add to baking dish with oil
5. Season with turmeric, pink sea salt & black pepper
6. Bake at 400 for 35-45 minutes (flipping 1 or 2 times)

Grass Fed Beef Roast

- 1 Organic grass fed beef roast
- 6-8 Red potatoes
- 2-4 Carrots (chop them)
- 1 Leek stalk
- 2 Cloves of garlic minced
- 1/3 Cup of organic pickle juice
- 1 Cup of bone broth
- Pink sea salt, pepper, turmeric and 2 TBSP of butter

1. Melt butter in a pan and brown the roast on both sides
2. Combine pickle juice, bone broth & leeks in crock pot
3. Add meat
4. Add carrots, potatoes & garlic
5. Spoon remaining butter over top
6. Season with turmeric, sea salt, black pepper
7. Cook on low for 6-8 hours

Heavenly PB & J Cups

- 1/3 Cup of natural peanut butter
- 1/3 Cup of coconut oil
- 1 Scoop vanilla protein powder
- 1 Cup frozen organic strawberries
- Raw macadamia, walnut & cashew mix

Peanut butter filling:

1. Melt coconut oil in sauce pan
2. Remove from heat, add natural peanut butter & vanilla protein powder and stir until mixed

Berry filling:

1. Heat berries in small saucepan, smashing them as they cook

Layer peanut butter, berries and more peanut butter in baking dish and top with crushed nuts

Place in refrigerator for 1-2 hours or until firm

Store in fridge

Grass Fed Avocado Burgers

- Grass fed burgers
- Cheese of your choice
- 1/3 Cup coconut aminos
- Garlic (1-2 cloves minced)
- Sprouted buns
- Avocado

1. Mix coconut aminos and minced garlic pour over burgers
2. Cook under broiler flipping as needed
3. Top with Cheese
4. Top with veggies and condiments of your choice

Crispy Fries

- Organic red potatoes
- Avocado oil
- Seasonings

1. Cut into thin round slices
2. Place single layer on oiled cookie sheet
3. Season
4. Bake at 350 turning 1-2 times until crispy

Cabbage Stir Fry

- 1 Head of cabbage chopped
- 2 Zucchini
- 1 Head of broccoli
- 2 Cups of spinach
- 2 TBSP Kerrygold butter

1. Add cabbage & broccoli with Kerrygold butter to skillet and brown cabbage

2. Add zucchini and spinach until slightly soft

3. Season with turmeric, pink sea salt & pepper

Cauliflower Rice

- Shredded cauliflower (1 bag)
- 2 Zucchini
- 4-6 Beet greens (leaves)
- Garlic (2 cloves)
- Leeks (1 stalk)
- Avocado oil

1. Chop zucchini, greens, leeks and garlic
2. Mix cauliflower, garlic & leeks in oil in skillet
3. Add zucchini
3. Season with turmeric, pink sea salt & black pepper
4. Sauté until brown and serve

Elderberry Syrup

"Our favorite natural immunity booster"

- ½ Cup organic, dried elderberries
- ½-1 Inch piece of fresh ginger root
- 4 Whole cloves
- 1 Cup raw/local honey
- 3 Cups water
- 1 Whole organic cinnamon stick
- 2 Whole chinese star anise

1. Pour water into medium saucepan.
2. Add elderberries, ginger, anise, cinnamon, cloves. (Do NOT add honey yet)
3. Bring to a boil then cover and simmer on low for 45 minutes to an hour (liquid reduces to ½)
4. Remove from heat and let cool enough to be handled
5. Pour through a strainer into a glass jar or bowl. Let cool to lukewarm.
6. Once it's cooled add honey and stir well
7. Pour into mason jar and store in refrigerator

Take 1x daily for immune boosting or every 2-3 hours if sick. Standard dose is ½-1 tsp for kids and 1 TBSP for adults

Sweet Potato Breakfast Bowl

- 1 Large cooked sweet potato
- 3-4 TBSP almond butter
- 3 TBSP almond milk
- Full fat coconut milk
- Blueberries
- Cinnamon
- 1 Scoop protein powder

1. Precook 4-5 sweet potatoes for the week.
2. Combine sweet potato, almond butter, protein powder, flax milk in blender and blend until smooth.

3. Pour in bowl and top with blueberries, coconut milk and cinnamon

Homemade Cleaning Spray

"A natural way to clean!"

- Large Mason Jar
- Organic white vinegar
- Organic orange peels
- Organic orange essential oil
- Organic Cleanse and Defence essential oils
- Organic cinnamon essential oil OR peppermint (these oils are great around the holidays)

1. Add orange peels from 2-3 oranges to mason jar

2. Fill jar to top with vinegar

3. Add 5-8 drops of orange essential oil

4. Add 3-5 drops of Cleanse and Defence essential oils. It it's around the holidays swap these out for cinnamon or peppermint essential oils

5. Let sit for 1 week, remove orange peels and pour into spray bottle

Natural Laundry Soap

I challenge you to look up the ingredients in your laundry soap! Try the app Think Dirty!

- 2 Gallon bucket
- 2 Gallons water
- 1/2 Cup Super-Washing Soda
- 1/2 Cup Baking Soda
- 1 ½ Cup castile soap (I use Dr. Bronner's in lavender)
- 30 Drops of your favorite essential oils (I use lavender, ylang ylang and lemon)
- Large wooden/plastic spoon to stir
- 2, 1-Gallon glass containers

1. **Add super washing soda to bucket and add about 3 inches water. Stir until dissolved**
2. **Add baking soda and stir until dissolved**
3. **Fill bucket to about an inch from the top**
4. **Add castile soap**
5. **Add essential oils**
6. **Transfer to storage container**

Use ⅓- ½ cup per load of laundry

"It's not easy getting the family to put their phones down and participate at dinner! We've found that including the kids in cooking helps them appreciate healthy food and enjoy our family dinner... they forget about their phones every time!"

Brandy

"Herbs are the friend of the physician and the pride of cooks" ~Charlemagne

"Mother Nature provides all the ingredients we need"

Shopping List

"The outer walls of a grocery store offer the purest foods. Stay out of the middle"

Shop local first if you can! Farmers markets are everywhere, you just have to look or ask around on Facebook! I try and purchase our eggs and meats from a local farm whenever possible and I only purchase local honey.

I can't stress enough how important it is to read labels!!! Look at where your food is coming from. Wild caught Salmon is great but not if it's coming from China!! Check for artificial flavors and ingredients and watch the sugar content!!

You want to steer clear of added sugars! If a product comes in a box and you can't pronounce half the ingredients put it back and step away from that shelf!!!

ALDI

- Wild caught Salmon from Canada
- Kerrygold butter
- Medjool dates
- Organic black beans
- Organic diced tomatoes
- Goat cheese
- Organic coconut oil
- Kerrygold cheeses, I use Blarney Castle and Aged Cheddar
- Frozen organic fruits
- Organic coffee beans
- Gluten free pretzel sticks
- Organic, unrefined coconut oil
- Sprouted bread

EARTHFARE

- SO Delicious coconut milk creamer
- SO Delicious coconut milk yogurt
- Earth Fare brand Almond Milk
- Green Valley Organics Lactose Free sour cream
- Bentonite Clay
- Sprouted corn tortillas
- Alvarado St. sprouted bagels
- Rebl Macha drink
- Organic Eggs
- Fresh made natural peanut butter
- Manuka Honey

TARGET
Udi's pizza crust

WHOLE FOODS
Organic Cavatelli
Organic Orzo

AMAZON
Nutribiotic Ascorbic Acid (Vitamin C)
Organic dried Elderberries
Organic Chinese Star Anise
Silicone baking molds

FRESHTYHME

- Organic whole chickens
- Organic produce
- Meal replacement powder/shakes
- Turmeric root
- Avocado oil
- Ginger root
- Organic eggs

Supplements...

I highly suggest supplementing for you and your family. The challenge is there are so many brands that it's hard to decide which is best for you. I've learned to read labels and check the sourcing of the ingredients. In our Healthy Hustlers group on FB we have functional medicine doctors and chiropractors who I turn to for advice on vitamins, probiotics etc. They even offer discounts on supplements to the members of our group!

A lot of people come to me with questions about essential oils, weight loss products, detox teas, energy products and more. Over the years I've put together a list of carefully selected products that I believe in and trust to use with my family!

I'm very big on products that are organic and have clean ingredients. For example the essential oils and skin care products I use are Certified Organic, Fair Trade and Cruelty Free. Did you know that there are over 1,400 banned cosmetic ingredients in Europe but the US has only partially restricted 11???

Please remember that I am not a doctor, I'm just a mom on a mission to keep my family healthy in this toxic world! Always consult your doctor before trying any new diets, vitamins or supplements.

To learn more about the products I use for my family please visit www.mbpowercouple.com

"As a first time mom Healthy Hustlers has been such an inspiration in creating a healthier lifestyle for my little ones and my family. From the simple easy to follow recipes to the natural home remedies, it has been a go to guide for me. I always look forward to reading the daily posts and learning more about healthy living." Little things like switching to pink salt and using turmeric. It's introduced us to veggies I didn't even know existed. One thing I love is it's taught me to pay more attention to labels and such! **Jessica Kincaid, Cuyahoga Falls Ohio**

Brandy Bright has been a true inspiration for healthy living. Her group page 'Healthy Hustlers' is a great network for likeminded people looking for inspiration to begin or encourage their healthy lifestyle. From the physical being to the mindset her desire to see others reach their goals is always the center of her focus. I'm blessed to be connected with such a 'Bright' beautiful soul that spreads light to everyone she meets. Keep sharing your amazing energy Brandy it's contagious and I'm totally hooked!
Rowena Yeager, Studio Wish Salon

These days, everyone is looking for a supplement to take to be healthy. The key to health lies not in a capsule, but rather right here in this book. Brandy Bright has put together nutritious, whole foods based meals that make eating healthy not only easy but delicious too!
Jerrica Sweetnich, ND, CNS

I've known Brandy for a number of years and she has certainly become my go to girl when it comes to living a healthy lifestyle and the best way to achieve it! Whether I have questions regarding vitamins, natural remedies or just some really yummy recipes she always has what I'm looking for. Brandy has inspired me to want to be the healthiest and best version of myself through her support, advice, and truly leading by example as she embodies what a "Healthy Hustler" really looks like inside and out!! **Ashley Collins, Fox SportsTime Ohio**

"Brandy is an incredible leader and fierce momma bear! She leads the health and wellness community by living out the wellness lifestyle for her own family including healthy eating, Chiropractic adjustments, essential oils, and so much more. Brandy and Mike have also built an incredible wellness community, the Healthy Hustlers, who unite around the empowering culture of wellbeing and vitality." **Dr. Kyle Wallner, Michigan Family Wellness PLLC**

Made in the USA
Lexington, KY
18 June 2018